We're **ready** for action and all **set** for fun.
Let's **GO** and get ready to play, everyone!

Warming up at the **track**, we stretch down to the ground,
Then get our hearts pumping by jogging around.

We line up in lanes, and then, ready, set… RUN!
We zoom to the finish! The race has begun.

Let's do **gymnastics** and fly through the air.
We tumble and cartwheel with power and flair.

We try to stay balanced and stick all our landings,
And cheer on our teammates for being outstanding!

Wearing our jerseys and **baseball** caps,
Each one of us takes a swing with the bat.

We send the ball flying and set a quick pace,
Working hard as we can to reach the next base.

We dive in the water and make a big splash!
Kicking fast with our legs, **swimming** by in a flash.

We work on our strokes in the glistening pool,
Then we rest and we float and the water feels cool.

Some call it **football** and some call it **soccer**.
The forwards love scoring; the goalie's the blocker.

We zip down the field as we kick at the ball,
Using feet, knees and bodies — but no hands at all!

It's time to play **hockey** — excitement awaits!
We put on our helmets and lace up our skates.

Skating the ice rink takes care and control.
We pass the puck down towards the other team's goal.

When we're at **karate**, our work is intense.
We learn self-control and we gain confidence.

From white belt to black belt, our skill slowly grows.
With focus and patience, we'll all feel like pros!

On the **basketball** court, the pace is quite fast.
When we hear *"I'm open!"*, we turn and we pass.

We dribble the ball and we work up a sweat.
We shoot and then — *swish!* It goes straight in the net!

All over the world, kids love to play.
What kind of **sport** will you try out today?

Track and Field

A running race was the only event at the first ancient Olympic Games in Greece! Today people in over 200 countries enjoy events like sprinting, hurdling and relay races, making track and field the second most popular sport in the world. Runners from East African nations like Kenya and Ethiopia hold many of the world records in track and field.

Gymnastics

Gymnasts perform acts of balance, strength and flexibility. They sometimes use equipment like a balance beam, which is a long, narrow beam raised off the floor. They perform for a panel of judges who give them a score based on how well they do their routines. Gymnastics is popular in Russia, Romania, China, the United States and beyond.

Baseball

In this team sport, players take turns striking a ball with a bat and then running around the field to all four bases to score. Baseball is the national sport of both Cuba and the United States, and also the most popular sport in Japan and Venezuela.

Swimming

Competitive swimming began in England, the home of the first public swimming pool. Swimmers compete with four different strokes or ways to swim — backstroke, breaststroke, butterfly and freestyle. People all around the world swim for fun and for sport. In Australia, almost half of all the people who live there consider themselves to be swimmers!

Football/Soccer

Whether you call it soccer or football, this sport is the most popular game in the world, played by people from more than 200 countries. Two teams of eleven players compete to get the ball past the goalkeeper into the other team's net without using their hands or arms.

Ice Hockey

In ice hockey, two teams of ice skaters score points by using sticks to shoot a rubber disk called a puck into the other team's net. Ice hockey is Canada's national sport, and the game is also popular in the United States as well as the cold climates of northern Europe.

Karate

Karate began in Japan but is now enjoyed by people all around the world. Karate involves learning a series of moves that are graded by teachers to earn different belts — starting from white and working up to black. The sport helps both mind and body by building strength and self-control.

Basketball

When basketball was first invented, it was played with a soccer ball and a peach basket! Now two teams of five players bounce an orange ball around the court, shooting it into a net basket to score points. Today basketball is the most popular sport in the Philippines.

To Mom & Dad,
for always cheering me on
— C. C.

For you, the reader of this book!
Stay awesome — C. E.

Barefoot Books
2067 Massachusetts Ave
Cambridge, MA 02140

Barefoot Books
29/30 Fitzroy Square
London, W1T 6LQ

First published in United States of America by Barefoot Books, Inc
and in Great Britain by Barefoot Books, Ltd in 2020
All rights reserved

Graphic design by Sarah Soldano, Barefoot Books
Edited and art directed by Kate DePalma, Barefoot Books
Reproduction by Bright Arts, Hong Kong
Printed in China on 100% acid-free paper
This book was typeset in Adriatic and Charter
The illustrations were prepared in acrylic,
water-based paints and digital collage

Hardback ISBN 978-1-78285-985-7
Paperback ISBN 978-1-78285-991-8
E-book ISBN 978-1-78285-997-0

British Cataloguing-in-Publication Data:
a catalogue record for this book is available
from the British Library

Library of Congress Cataloging-in-Publication Data
is available under LCCN 2019043262

1 3 5 7 9 8 6 4 2

The publisher would like to thank
the many expert reviewers who helped
ensure the accuracy of this book, including
school wellness researcher Scott Greenspan
and inclusivity specialist Anne Cohen.

Barefoot Books
step inside a story

At Barefoot Books, we celebrate art and story that opens the hearts and minds of children from all walks of life, focusing on themes that encourage independence of spirit, enthusiasm for learning and respect for the world's diversity. The welfare of our children is dependent on the welfare of the planet, so we source paper from sustainably managed forests and constantly strive to reduce our environmental impact. Playful, beautiful and created to last a lifetime, our products combine the best of the present with the best of the past to educate our children as the caretakers of tomorrow.

www.barefootbooks.com

Celeste Cortright cartwheeled, swam, sprinted and jumped through her youth in Connecticut, USA. Today she lives in the city of Boston, Massachusetts, where she works as a design director and enjoys trying out different athletic activities. Celeste has also written *The More We Get Together* for Barefoot Books.

During her childhood in northern Germany, **Christiane Engel** tried out lots of sports, from gymnastics to tennis to judo to skateboarding. These days, she enjoys yoga, slow running and cycling in southeast England, where she lives and works as an author and illustrator. Christiane has illustrated several projects for Barefoot Books, including *Baby's First Words* and *Dump Truck Disco*.